PROUD

- Achieving Customer Service Excellence

Probably the only Customer Service acronym you will ever need

John Smart

Copyright © John Smart 2014
All rights reserved.

ISBN: 1499753772
ISBN 13: 978-1499753776

John Smart has asserted his rights under the Copyright, Designs, and Patents Act, 1988, and its amendments, to be identified as the author of this work.

Acknowledgements

I would like to dedicate this book first and foremost to my wife, Julie, for the undeniable dedication, love, and support she has given me during our married life. I would also like to include my children—Jennifer, Dominic, and Nieve—and in special memory of James.

Contents

Preface — vii

Chapter 1
Customer Service: From Bad to Good to Excellent — 1

Chapter 2
P: Polite and Professional — 23

Chapter 3
R: Respect — 31

Chapter 4
O: Own — 37

Chapter 5
U: Understand — 53

Chapter 6
D: Deliver — 73

Chapter 7
Be PROUD: *Achieving Excellent Customer Service*   **81**

About the author: 85

Appendix   87

Preface

*P*roud {adjective}: *feeling deep pleasure or satisfaction as a result of one's own achievements, qualities, or possessions or those of someone with whom one is closely associated.*
   Origin: late Old English prūt, prūd 'having a high opinion of one's own worth', from Old French 'prud', 'valiant', based on Latin prodesse 'be of value'.
   Oxford English Dictionary (2014)

Proud: one of the most emotive adjectives in the English language. *Proud to be black. Proud to be gay. Proud to be British.* These are just a few of the statements that we hear or see utilising the power of this single word to its full effect. *Proud* is the action hero in the adjective family: righting the wrong, championing the underdog, and rescuing other mere words and phrases, turning them into grateful participants who feel honoured to be standing shoulder to shoulder in the same statement or sentence.

Even on its own, the word makes an undeniable statement. Everyone who reads or hears it knows there is intention, a belief, a personal emotive investment. It shouts at you in an assertive yet inoffensive way. It makes you automatically sit up and take note. *Proud!*

From an individual, personal perspective, if you ever had to choose a word that expressed utter joy at your own achievement or to praise another for the same, then the word of choice is 'proud': *I'm so proud of you today. You made me proud. I'm so proud to have achieved this. Make me proud!* No other word can compete.

What has this to do with achieving customer service excellence? Everything. The tools contained in this book will highlight the importance, as well as the simplicity, of an acronym built around the powerful word PROUD. You will see how PROUD will build into a framework that, taken holistically, will provide a credible process to encompass your own personal, as well as organisational, ethos in providing excellent customer service. You shall see how, by adopting the spirit of PROUD, you will be able to use this as a basic tool in order to reach and maintain excellent customer service, and how this will become a standard that you will want others to adopt. Its simplicity, its ease of learning and understanding, will make its acceptance effortless. However—and this needs to be stressed at the outset—it is not a panacea for all customer service ills. It has to be used in context. To achieve this there has to be awareness, as well as individual responsibility, in ensuring that it is employed correctly.

This book is for anyone who deals with customers or has any form of customer interaction. That means all of us! At some time in our life, we will be a customer; we will also at some time need to deal with a customer.

Customer service, getting it right and doing it well, has never been more important than in today's unstable economy.

Preface

In the business word, the old adage that 'without customers we wouldn't be in business' is stronger now than it's ever been. Despite this relatively common-sense saying, many organisations, as well as individuals, fail to fully appreciate this fundamental aspect. Getting customer service right can mean the difference between failed, mediocre, and exceptional organisations.

When developing a customer service–focused culture within an organisation, there are a number of factors that need to be taken into account to satisfy the end user. The end user can range from the individual who has to implement and deliver the customer service, to the wider holistic organisational entity. The key components that have to be met include:

- Ease of use
- Practicality
- Simplicity
- Memorability

In addition there has to be acceptance: the end user has to be comfortable that the technique, process, model, theory, acronym, or other form makes sense. The methodology must be understood, that it can and will work, and be able to buy into it fully.

Using practical language, references to other models, common human behaviours, and examples, among other factors, PROUD can demonstrate that it meets the main criteria required by end users.

The aim of this book is not to teach you interpersonal tips and techniques in how to speak to customers, effectively handle customers, deal with their complaints, or negotiate; these topics are better serviced in other dedicated books or training workshops. I will not use undisputable data, graphs, charts, or statistics; nor will the concept profess to be a purely academic, scientific, or theoretical based model.

What I aim to do is to equip you with a memorable acronym that will serve you well in achieving excellent customer service, which, if adopted by the whole organisation, can provide a unified, simple, customer service–focused culture. The uniqueness of PROUD is that it can be used as an individual template, but at the same time it can be adapted and integrated holistically as a key part of an organisation's mission statement, communication, and culture. Like the word on which it is based, the model is not discriminatory—it can apply to any sector, discipline, or profession, to any individual or group.

The book will take you through the PROUD journey, its inception, and its relatedness in providing a framework for achieving excellent customer service. You will learn how each letter of PROUD builds up to embody the power, emotive aspects, and semantics of the word it is based on. Again, the formation of the PROUD model is not based on large, quantitated academic research, data, or long-term corporate studies; it is based on life experience, literature reviews, attendance and delivery at many different customer service–genre workshops, and human behaviour—with a sprinkling of common sense.

Another important point to note is that PROUD is not a step process. A process is something that is usually done in order, and typically only when one part is complete can you move on to the next. This is not the way with PROUD; each principle meshes and influences the next as well as others. While the intention would primarily be to start with 'P', you will see that, for example, 'P' shouldn't end when you go on to 'R'. Both should continue and be sustained throughout the customer service experience.

PROUD is a methodology, a philosophy of customer service that translates to being **Polite** and **Professional** at all times, having **Respect** for the customer; taking **Ownership** of the problem; gaining an **Understanding** of a customer's needs and wants; and ensuring you **Deliver** on what is possible.

When you have read through this book, you will gain a better appreciation and understanding of the PROUD principles and model; it will become apparent that 'its sum is greater than its individual parts' in achieving excellent customer service.

Chapter 1

Customer Service: From Bad to Good to Excellent

> 'People will forget what you said, people will forget what you did, but people will never forget how you made them feel.'
>
> *Maya Angelou, American author and poet (1928–2014)*

How many times have you had a poor customer service experience? Perhaps more than you care to mention. Think of one example now. Thinking about it? Good. The mere memory of a personal example starts to invoke the feelings and emotions that you probably felt at the time. Perhaps these were anger, frustration, or complete amazement that you were being treated so poorly. On the other end of the spectrum, how many times have you had a really good customer experience? Again, take a moment and think of one. Now, when you think about this specific example, your thoughts go down a different route: perhaps joy, due to the fact that you were being listened to and taken account of, and you feel at ease and more relaxed. It's amazing how customer experiences—both good and bad—can still evoke such strong emotions within people, even after considerable time has passed. Yet despite this, with all the customer service knowledge and investment in training and development conducted within organisations, poor customer service still exists.

What is a customer?

Before we go any further, we first need to define what we mean by a customer. In general terms, a customer is sometimes defined as being 'internal' or 'external'. The descriptor of an internal customer is usually given as the people you may deal with within your organisation. These may include, for example, your peers and colleagues, or people in other departments and sectors within the organisation (for example, the finance, HR, marketing, sales, and engineering departments).

The other type or class of customer is the external customer. This includes the traditional views of a customer: the suppliers, clients, members, patients, government bodies, agencies, or similar who are external to the normal organisational working environment. In both cases, internal and external, these will be individuals or sectors/departments that you deal with to possibly buy, sell, rent, or negotiate for a product or service. Therefore, whether it is internal or external customers you deal with, you will be providing a product or service. The product or service may be further categorised as either 'tangible' or 'intangible'. Using generalisation, tangible products are physical products or outputs produced; they can be touched, felt, and seen. Intangible products are usually classed as skills, expertise, or emotional and behavioural outputs that aren't physical—these may be advice, guidance, or information, for example. So, in essence, we have two classes of customer, internal and external, and customers are provided with a product or service, which can be tangible or intangible.

While we have defined what we mean by 'a customer', it's very important not to just think of the classic customer in a shop or customer service call centre scenario when reading this book. All the information provided regarding PROUD applies to the broad definition of a customer—which can easily include the interpersonal relationship between you and another person. As you gain an understanding of PROUD, you will clearly see that it can apply to any form of customer, in any context.

Customer satisfaction

Having defined the context and definition of a customer, we need to focus on the factors required to achieve excellent customer service. One important area is customer satisfaction. We can easily make the statement 'Customer service will influence customer satisfaction'. Logically, better service should mean better satisfaction and vice versa. This conjecture and other aspects are reflected in Kano's customer satisfaction model.

Kano's customer satisfaction model

In the 1980s, Noriaki Kano, professor emeritus of the Tokyo University of Science, developed his model of customer satisfaction. There are many other models and theories in this area, but this model is probably the most widely used and easily understood. References to this model will further help support the flexibility and holistic use of PROUD in relation to the customer satisfaction levels described by Kano, which are now adopted in general use.

Kano's model offers some insight into the perceived attributes important to customers. It is used to provide better understanding of products and services by way of where they are on the model, and to highlight any appropriate action needed. His model focuses on differentiating product features, as opposed to focusing initially on customer needs, but it can indicate where customer satisfaction lies.

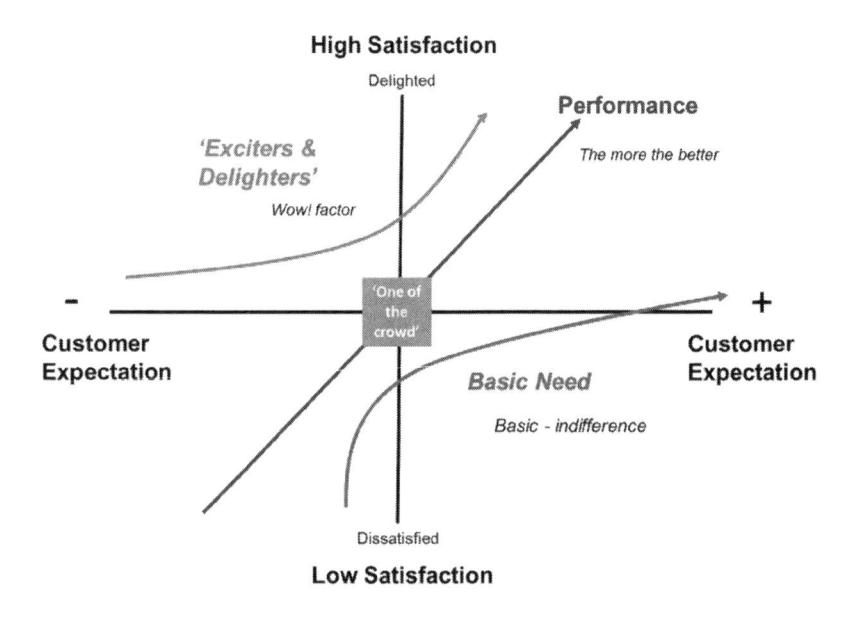

Figure 1. Example of Professor Kano's customer satisfaction model.

Kano's model is a graph, which consists of a horizontal and a vertical axis. The vertical axis relates to the satisfaction level; the horizontal axis originally related to customer expectation or implementation. However, its use, like that of all models, has been adapted and interpreted to suit many situations, and you will sometimes see this horizontal line in a quality context, or performance context, or other forms. Generally, the graph is interpreted in this way:

'Exciters and Delighters'—the wow factor

At or above this curve, these attributes provide high satisfaction when achieved fully, but their absence does not lead to dissatisfaction. These are attributes that are not normally expected, but when included, they will exceed the customer's expectations and can contribute to high levels of customer satisfaction.

For example, when BlackBerry first incorporated e-mail on their mobile devices, this was a 'wow' factor. The BlackBerry quickly became the mobile media device of many business people. This ensured the market share for BlackBerry at the time. These types of attributes of quality unexpectedly delight customers. Sometimes they are often unspoken, and it's the act of a bold genius that brings these to the forefront. As Henry Ford is reputed to have once said, 'If I had asked people what they wanted, they would have said faster horses.' Another example is Steve Jobs with the Apple iPad. The danger is that today's 'exciter' or unique selling point (USP) becomes tomorrow's basic need, as per the BlackBerry and iPad example. Now all mobile smartphones are e-mail enabled, and the tablet computer is becoming more commonplace. So organisations need to be constantly monitoring this area to ensure that their unique selling point or exciter remains fresh.

Performance—a linear attribute: 'the more the better'

Performance attributes are those for which more is generally better and will improve customer satisfaction. These attributes result in increased satisfaction when fulfilled and dissatisfaction when not fulfilled. These are attributes that are spoken of and verbalised by customers. This area provides the cornerstone of all customer-focused training—for example, 'Dissatisfied customers will tell three other people of their experience; satisfied customers will tell ten'. These attributes are the ones that companies compete for, and they form the weighted needs against which product concepts will be evaluated. There is also a direct correlation between these performance attributes and the price that a customer is willing to pay for a product. Customers are willing to pay more for a product or service that will provide more than the standard. An example of this would be paying a higher premium for individual customer service and prompt response when dealing with complaints, as well as extremely helpful staff. If this service is maintained, then customers will accept the extra cost, being satisfied with the service; if not maintained, then they will be dissatisfied. In both cases, they are likely to voice their views to others, whether these are positive or negative.

Basic/threshold needs

These attributes are taken for granted when fulfilled but may result in dissatisfaction when not fulfilled. Increasing the performance of these attributes may provide diminishing returns in terms of customer satisfaction; however, the absence or poor performance of these attributes may result in extreme customer dissatisfaction. An example of this would be the packaging of a carton of juice. The basic requirement is that the carton won't leak. Customers are dissatisfied when the package leaks, but when it does not leak, the result is not increased customer satisfaction, as this was a basic expectation. Since customers expect these attributes and view them as basic, it is unlikely that they are going to tell the company about them when asked, for example, 'Great packaging, doesn't leak'. The more likely comment would be 'Great packaging, easy to handle' or 'Great packaging; the bold, bright colours stand out'.

There are other things to note as well:

Neutral attributes—indifference

These attributes refer to aspects that are neither good nor bad, and they do not result in either customer satisfaction or customer dissatisfaction.

Reverse expectations

These attributes refer to a high degree of achievement resulting in dissatisfaction and to the fact that not all customers are alike. For example, some customers prefer high-tech products, while others prefer the basic model of a product and will be dissatisfied if a product has too many extra features.

Kano's model is not the only theory of the changing face of customer satisfaction, but it's a good model that highlights some important points. The model can provide the framework (that is, basic performance, and delight) and a barometer with which we can assess, monitor, and evaluate customer satisfaction, assessing products and innovations. It can be used as a strategic model to review and think about how to attract or keep customers: how to analyse what they want, what they need, and what you can give them. It helps to keep a watch on the delight; if your product or service becomes staid, then look for alternatives or new experiences. It can be used operationally to show where complacency issues may arise with performance and to formulate plans to overcome these. When used in workshops and team situations, it can create debate and aid the generation of new ideas and concepts.

The examples given help to explain the model with product innovations, but what is the relationship between the model and customer service? For example, what about the other products and services, the ones that, even with or without extras and 'delighters', still maintain a strong market share through a solid base of repeat customers? There are many companies around that have produced the same product with little or no change through generations of ownership and are still going strong. There are many examples where the basic shape, components, and build of products have been the same for many years, from tailors, to shoes, to furniture, to cookers. The only changes have been made mainly because of regulatory or sustainability requirements, rather than customers being dissatisfied with the product.

So it's not just about changing products or services to interest or 'wow' customers to remain loyal. There are other considerations. Many of these traditional or historic firms have kept a loyal customer base not just because of the product but also because of the service. The way that the customer is treated is vitally important. Kano's model can easily be transposed into providing a basic framework for customer service excellence. It can demonstrate this, for example, by satisfying the three main areas: basic needs (polite and professional service), performance (the more you do, the better, or going that extra mile), and the delighters (the unexpected touch, for example, the chocolate on the pillow, the bunch of flowers on the front seat of the new car when the salesperson hands you the keys).

But unfortunately it's not as simple as that. An assumption is made that, for example, everyone will like a chocolate on his or her pillow, whereas with customer service, there are other factors that we need to take into account, predominately about understanding the needs of the customer. So, while PROUD uses Kano's model as an important guide and reference to help explain the context of interaction within the three areas, it considers further the human behaviours and interpersonal relationships within the customer service experience.

Human factors

The majority of customer interaction involves a human-to-human interface. We are simple yet, at the same time, complex beings. This paradigm in itself causes problems, as there will be generalised as well as specific statements made in this area, and these need to be addressed in the context they are in. Even in the other cases of non-human-to-human interaction (for example, direct entry on an Internet web page), there are human factors that need to be considered—for example, if the web page is too complicated and not user friendly, then it will not meet the satisfaction of the customer.

Perception

One area that has an influence and bearing on human behaviour is perception. Perception is an important aspect when dealing with a customer, and it's an area that is often overlooked during customer engagement.

Perception, in a generalised context, involves taking in sensory information in order to form an opinion about something. Basically, sensory information involves the five senses of taste, touch, smell, hearing, and sight, or a combination of these. Perception is usually simplified down to your take on things, or how you view something. We tend to use sensory words; for example, in the case of 'view something', we may actually mean this not in the pure sense of vision, but in the sense of the construct of your perception. For example, my view of a house will be different from your view of the same house. It's still the same house, but you will see it in a different context. These differences may be subtle, or they may be large. You may see quaint, rustic charm where I see lots of remedial maintenance. You may see a large, rolling garden where I see summers of constant mowing.

It's important to be aware of perception, as it can be formed well before you have any personal interaction with the customer, like in the case of prior exposure to media, communication, adverts, and so on. With personal engagement, in general, a person will form a perception (opinion) about someone within the first thirty seconds of contact (for example, upon hearing or seeing a person, or even reading a CV), and this perception will then be further confirmed, reinforced, or discarded within the next two to three minutes. Once this perception has been formed in the mind of the individual, it will take more effort to change it. First impressions count.

In a lot of customer-focused literature, workshops, and programmes, you will often hear or see the statement 'Put yourself in the shoes of the customer' or 'You should treat others as you yourself would want to be treated'. The intention is to try to perceive what it's like for the customer and, in that situation, to question whether you would accept the same. These are good maxims to follow, to some degree, but certainly not a panacea that can be applied at all times.

Part of the reason is that it's sometimes difficult to actually perceive something in the same way as another person. Perception is about interpreting the data and making sense of it in context of what we already know. It's personal. If I have never had an experience in a particular situation, then I may find it difficult to *perceive* what it's actually like for an individual who has. Each of us has varying perspectives on a range of topics, from politics to life, from tastes to people. Just because one person likes a certain type of food doesn't mean that everyone will; if some have a certain belief in something and you don't, then they (and you) will have different perspectives. In customer service, where one person may be happy to accept a certain level of customer service, it may be less than what another would expect.

This can equally occur in the perspectives between customers and organisations. As an example, if you were to ask customers what would be the ideal customer service solution for them, their response may be to have a personalised, bespoke, or customised service. However, if you were to ask organisations this question, from their perspective they may say they would like a 'magic bullet', a one-size-fits-all, cost-neutral solution. It can then become very difficult to 'put yourself in the shoes of the customer' if an organisation delivers a standard service and the customer's perception is to have a bespoke service.

Therefore, it's important to establish or set the perception of the customer as soon as possible and in the correct context, as this will have bearing on the whole customer experience. Or, if the perception has already been formed, then you need to understand what it is. Through this understanding you will be able to adapt your approach accordingly. We will look further at this concept within the PROUD principles later in the book.

Another key part to understanding perception and how it links in with the PROUD model is expectation.

Expectation

Often aligned with perception is expectation. Expectation is defined as having a strong belief that something will happen, either now, in the present, or in the future. This belief is created or influenced by our perception of the information we have. For example, I see an advert for a job. Having read the job description (sensory input), I form a general opinion as to whether I want to apply for the job. (Others read the advert and decide it's not for them—a difference in perspective.) In the advert I see 'includes company vehicle, phone, and laptop'. My perception (opinion) may be 'I like the idea of that. Looks like a good company with some good benefits', which in turn guides my expectation (belief) where I may see myself with a top-of-the-range, high-end executive vehicle and state-of-the-art phone and laptop. However, during the interview, it becomes very clear that there is a large discrepancy between my expectation and reality. The vehicle is a bicycle, and the phone and laptop are outdated.

It's this discourse between perception, expectation, and reality that is the cause of most customer service problems. As another example, if you were to see a hotel advertised as 'five-star', your perception would be that it is a high-end establishment. Your expectation would be to have excellent food, attentive service, first-rate facilities, and so on. If, in reality, the service, location, and food are poor, then your expectation, which was influenced by your perception, has not been met.

The important point to realise is that it's not just the expectation that you need to take into account—it's also what formed the customer's initial perception. Perception influences expectation. If the wrong perception has been set, then the customer will create the wrong expectation.

Virtues

We have seen that the general statement 'You should treat others as you yourself would like to be treated' is a favourable maxim among customer service exponents, albeit with a small caveat. If, however, this was changed into a question, it would be 'How exactly would you like to be treated?' You will then hear statements that will contain the key virtues deemed to be important to providing excellent customer service, and typically, these will be virtues common to the majority of people: 'I want to be treated with…. I need the person to show…. I would ideally like….' The common missing words include these:

- Trust
- Honesty
- Openness
- Integrity
- Respect

There may be one or two more to add, but, in essence, these are the key wants and needs that the individual, company, or organisation the customer is dealing with has to demonstrate or provide. These are borne from internal virtues and external beliefs, as well as other emotional human aspirations. These are the key intangible qualities that distinguish excellent customer service from good or mediocre customer service.

Getting these right will ensure that, despite the market sector you operate in, you will retain, sustain, and more than likely grow your customer base as needed. It is these general yet widely under-addressed basic human principles that are lacking in customer service situations, even from some of the more upmarket, exclusive companies. However, we cannot talk about basic human principles aligned to customer service without gaining an understanding of the basic theories of human motivation.

Motivation and behaviour

A basic definition of motivation is the process that initiates, guides, and maintains goal-oriented behaviours. Basically, it is what causes us to act, whether that act is getting food to reduce hunger or reading a book to gain knowledge.

In essence it involves the biological, emotional, social, and cognitive forces that activate behaviour. Generally, in everyday usage, the term 'motivation' is used to describe why a person does something.

Within us all we have many motivators, needs, and wants. Taking the most common theories around this area from the likes of Maslow, Herzberg, Vroom, and Alderfer as examples, and grouping these into a simplified model, it can be seen that there are basically three common areas that we share:

- **Survival:** We all have the will to live. You will do what is necessary to survive; for example, if you fall into the sea, you will fight to stay afloat. If someone grabs you around the throat, you will try to fend your attacker off. Alternatively, the situation may require you to get away from the danger or take evasive action if the threat is too severe (the ingrained 'fight-or-flight' response).

- **Social interaction:** All humans need social interaction, affection, and a sense of belonging. As with many things, the degree of need is different in us all. For example, you may classify some people as loners, but to them, they have enough interaction to satisfy their needs. In a sense, this is why solitary confinement can be deemed a punishment.

- **Achievement:** All humans have a desire to succeed, to achieve something. Here again, the actual degree of success and what this means is different in us all. To some, winning the race gives the sense of achievement; to others, just being able to take part in the race is an achievement in itself.

What has all of this to do with customer excellence? Again, a lot. If you look at the first area, the survival aspect, if we feel that we are being threatened, however slight, then we will take what we deem to be the appropriate action. This is sometimes simplified as the fight-or-flight response: we will either confront the problem or retreat from it. The same basic responses can manifest when we feel we are being treated badly—for example, when we receive poor customer service. There may not be any physical threat, but there is a challenge to our personal integrity, honour, or self-respect, which can be seen as equally damaging. Some people will retaliate, adopting a fight response through anger, frustration, disgust, raising their voice, and adopting aggressive body language. All of this may drive further resistance or retaliation, leading to a possible escalating spiral of bad behaviours from both parties. On the other hand, we may demonstrate a flight response by walking away from the situation or acting subdued, but in doing so, we may feel bitter or disappointed with the way we were treated, which may then further manifest as resentment.

Take the second common trait, social interaction, as another example, and apply this to the interaction we have as a customer, and it soon becomes clear that this is an area where we want to be treated fairly and respectfully and listened to. In other words, we want to be liked, and having a poor customer service experience goes against this basic need. We may take the fact that we have not been treated fairly or with the degree of respect that we feel appropriate as a personal slight or insult.

As for the third area, achievement, again this may be sensed when we have received, or have given, good customer service. This can invoke a feeling of pleasure or well-being. In a customer service context, we want the transaction to be completed smoothly, without stress, and with some sense of satisfaction, a pleasurable feeling; we want the transaction to be something we would be more than happy to do again. This sense of achievement—that is, having done something well or received something good—is one of the mainstays of excellent customer service.

We can now appreciate that customer service involves or is strongly influenced by behavioural and motivational factors. The PROUD model encompasses all of these key behavioural areas as an integral part of its structure. More importantly, when PROUD is fully applied, it can create the right conditions to provide positive outcomes and alleviate any negative consequences.

Keep it simple

As stated earlier in this chapter, we are simple yet complex beings. We have complexity in cognitive functions, behaviour, feelings, emotions, and perceptions—yet we are simple in that we share some common traits and behaviours. We are a cybernetic system, where the complexities of the mind and body are congruent, performing millions of internal microprocessing actions, but where the inputs are preferred to be simple. Too much sensory information, for example, can confuse us to the extent that the information is useless as it cannot be processed correctly.

In 1956, the cognitive psychologist George A. Miller of Princeton University produced his report[1] highlighting the relative capacity for remembering information. His experiments identified that we are capable of remembering seven items, plus or minus two, when shown them. This is often referred to as 'Miller's Law'. The 'magical number seven', which Miller used only as a rhetorical term, has been open to some debate, with other experiments highlighting the numbers four through eight depending on the items—for example, musical notes, words, or numbers. Whatever the magical number is, what all of this shows is that we have a general limited capacity to take in information we are presented with.

You've probably experienced this yourself when being asked to remember a phone number in one go or a list of things to get from the shop. So if we want people to remember something, then it's far better to adopt the old principle 'KISS—Keep it Simple Stupid' or alternatively 'KISS - Keep it Simple and Straightforward'.

Therefore, the message from the organisation, whether this is the customer vision, mission statement, policy, or customer essential message, has to be clear, simple, and understood. The KISS method of 'Keep It Simple…' is key. As the acronym

---

1 'The Magical Number Seven, Plus or Minus Two: Some limits on our capacity for processing information' –Miller, G.A., *Psychological Review*, 1956

'PROUD' consists of five letters, each having pertinent meaning, collectively forming a memorable word, it applies the KISS principle and aligns with Miller's Law.

In addition to ensuring that the message is kept clear, concise, and understood, there has to be a belief, 'the buy-in', that it does work. It has to be pragmatic, easily remembered, and adopted. If you are responsible for performing, then you have to be comfortable that you can work with the method in order for the task to be achieved. Communication, workshops, or programmes that try to embody false behaviours or terms that wouldn't naturally be said never work well. The person undergoing this training feels uncomfortable adapting to this way of working; it's not natural or typical behaviour, and it shows.

Integrated into all of these ideas within this first chapter are some of the real keys to providing the basis to achieve excellent customer service. What are they, and how can they be formulated into a simple construct that is understood and accepted by the majority of people who have to implement it? It will be shown over the course of this book how PROUD aims to satisfy the requirements of a simple, pragmatic, effective acronym that embodies the general theories and models associated with providing excellent customer service.

Summary

This opening chapter has provided some general information about the definitions, beliefs, experiences, theories, models, and statements surrounding the topic of customer service. It's important to have an appreciation of these in order to understand how they relate and influence customer service, customer interaction, and customer satisfaction. Perception, expectation, basic needs, delighters, or motivators—they all play a part in the overall customer experience (whichever side of the experience you are on and with whatever customer definition you are applying it to).

What do Maya Angelou's quote at the beginning of this chapter, your own thoughts and examples of good and bad customer experiences, Kano's model, and the broad overview of human behaviours have in common? They all highlight that one of the key areas in providing excellent customer service involves how you make people feel. This entails understanding and defining people's perceptions, expectations, and behaviours to ensure that you deal with them correctly and appropriately, addressing their intrinsic needs of trust, openness, and respect.

You have also seen that one of the vital points for achieving engagement with people in delivering excellent customer focus within an organisation is to keep it simple, in a language or style that can be understood at all levels.

You will see, as you read through the rest of the book, how PROUD supplements and supports these areas to provide a workable, pragmatic solution. In the course of this book, you will understand how PROUD does all of the following:

- Serves as a model in helping to provide the principles to help achieve excellent customer service
- Has no boundary with regard to customer definition or scope—it can be utilised by all classes, sectors, and professions
- Can be utilised on an individual basis, as well as adopted and used at organisational level as part of its mission statement, vision, or corporate communication
- Encompasses and addresses the virtues deemed important to the customer
- Addresses expectations by helping in setting the perception
- Takes into consideration human behaviour and motivational aspects, aligned to customer service interaction
- Incorporates and highlights the key levels of Kano's customer satisfaction model—basic need, performance, and delighters—through its use
- Is formed from individual words, each with meaning and relevance to customer service
- Forms one of the most powerful and emotive words in the English language
- Is simple, memorable, and easily understood

PROUD is not some highly complex theoretical model; its aim is to provide a simple, pragmatic, easily understood base for achieving excellent customer service.

An inherent benefit of PROUD is that it is not just about dealing with customer-focused situations but about dealing with people in general. It is a conceptual model that applies to both business and personal life effortlessly. By adopting PROUD in your personal life as well as your business life, you will enhance not only your everyday customer experience but your life experience as well.

Chapter 2

P: Polite and Professional

'What does it cost to say "thank you"? What does it cost to say "please"? You know my name, so why not use it?'

Polite

Even the very word 'polite' conjures up visions of a bygone era of impeccable behaviour, whereby people tried hard to appease others through implied mutual respect. It's not a recent nineteenth or even twentieth-century concept; its etymological origin can be dated as far back as the thirteenth century, probably derived by the Latin 'polītus', past participle of 'polīre', meaning 'to polish', and taken as a word to describe 'elegant' or 'refined'. However, politeness itself, its meaning, and its uses can be further extended back many hundreds of years through Asian cultures, especially in China and Japan. It has to be noted that 'polite', or politeness, is in fact culture-bound—what may appear to be polite in one culture may in fact be impolite in another. So when addressing the aspect of being polite, be fully aware of any applicable cultural differences, as these will have to be taken in context of one's own environment and culture.

Being polite is usually portrayed as the showing of good manners—that is, being courteous and respectful of the other person as well as putting others' feelings and needs first. Conducted correctly, it can invoke good feelings in the person receiving, as well as a sense of well-being in the person giving. This harks back to the virtuous statement of 'It is better to give than to receive'. However, if politeness is taken to the extreme, it can actually have the opposite effect. An example of this is sometimes portrayed in the classic comedy sketch where, having opened the door, one person invites the other to go first; however, also wishing to appear polite, the other repays the compliment by requesting the same. This exchange of pleasantries continues for some time; neither person is willing to going through for fear of being seen as impolite. Eventually, losing patience with each other, they start to argue, thereby turning good manners on its head.

While this example highlights one end of the extreme, the other end (that is, a complete lack of politeness or good manners) can instantaneously evoke very strong feelings of anger or frustration. Terms like 'ignorant' or 'rude' are generally used (among others), as well as displays of retaliation, disgust, or horror. So, why does the lack of politeness or good manners invoke these feelings within us?

Politeness, and indeed good manners, operates on the basic requirements of human behaviour, which include the behaviours associated with motivation, among others. As a reminder,

P: Polite and Professional

we have already seen that these can be highlighted under three main areas: survival, social interaction, and achievement.

The act of being polite to another person can satisfy the social and the achievement aspect, as well as, it can be argued, that of survival: 'If the other person likes me, then they are less likely to do me harm or to get me into a dangerous situation.'

We are individuals, and we want to be treated as special or unique but, at the same time, still feel part of the whole. Whether this recognition is in the form of praise or acknowledgement, it is a basic requirement that, if not satisfied, can lead to a certain degree of personal dissatisfaction. If recognition is not received, this may contribute to feeling distant from the other person, as well as promote other neutral or negative emotions and feelings. This in turn can hinder or prevent any further development from gaining acceptable rapport, which may in turn damage relationship building.

One of the basic components of recognition (and an important key) is using and calling someone by his or her name, preferably a first name. Understandably, in some customer-focused situations, like the first contact with the customer, it may be seen to be a little too familiar to suddenly use someone's first name. So the immediate response is to use 'sir', 'madam', or a status and surname, such as 'Mrs Smith' or 'Professor Johnson'.

The main point to remember is that whenever possible, you should ensure that you use a person's name. Ideally, let the other person know yours first, and then find out the other person's. This is not a hard thing to do. It doesn't take a lot to say 'I'm sorry, I didn't quite get your name' or 'I'm sorry, we don't seem to have been introduced; my name is John. What's yours?' Once you have a name, use it! How many times have you felt that you were being listened to when someone used your name and sprinkled it into the conversation? As always, here the key is to apply the 'Goldilocks principle'—not too much and not too little, but just enough to keep interest, to let the person know that you are treating him or her as an individual.

Another aspect of being polite that is often overlooked is the ability to say 'thank you'. The old adage that a thank-you costs nothing but is priceless to those receiving it is something that should never be forgotten. Manners, good manners, are sometimes a rarity these days. It may be owing to the changing generations, the loss of more engaged social interaction and guidance, or that etiquette is being viewed as slightly outdated. Despite these encroaching views, you need to remember that it is our own human behaviour that wants and needs this recognition—so don't ignore it.

Professional

Taken literally, a professional is a member of a profession. Generally, if the profession has an affiliated membership, then one of the things that binds the professional members together is a code of ethics or guidelines that stipulate how they should conduct themselves within that profession. One of the most well known code of ethics is the Hippocratic Oath.

However, it does not take an affiliated membership or organisation to imply that people, when conducting their particular line of business or commercial undertakings, should abide by certain implied, unwritten ethics and codes of conduct. For example, a waiter in a restaurant may not belong to any union or professional affiliated body, but there will be both implied and explicit expectations that they are conducting their work professionally. Again, from the Kano principle, there will be basic expectations (clean, presentable, polite), and then there will be performance expectations (attentive, engaging, knowledgeable of the menu/wine list), then delighters (providing you the best seat in the restaurant). Only when a waiter, in this example, transcends basic expectations into the performance attributes and above would you really start to notice or comment that they are being professional in their work. So even if there is no official professional body that the person belongs to, society may have laid down unwritten, implied standards, codes, and ethics that people should follow if they want to be deemed to be acting professionally.

Being professional in your particular discipline or vocation may involve you looking at the professional body's code of conduct, ethics, and standards and reviewing them against your own behaviours. If there is no affiliated body, then seek other sources of information; for example, find vocational qualifications in that subject area's literature or speak with other colleagues as well as your customers. Be aware that, like a lot of things, 'professional' can mean different things to different people, and what one person deems as being professional may not necessarily be right.

This leads into one of the best-known maxims in the customer service world: 'The customer is always right.' But is this true? This phrase was reputed to have been coined in the early part of the twentieth century, originating from the large emerging hotel chains and retail department stores. The idea was, for example, if a customer complained that the soup was too cold, it should be removed immediately and fresh soup be brought out; no questions, no quibbles. This is excellent customer service, but the maxim, even then, was never to be taken as absolute, the caveat being that there were, at times, unscrupulous customers who could push and test this statement.

Therefore, when being professional, there may come a point when you are being asked to conduct yourself, alone or on the part of an organisation, in ways that go against the code of ethics or moral standards. You may need to adapt the maxim to end with '…but even right can sometimes be wrong'. Another turn on this that I came across is '…but not right for us'. No one would expect you to bankrupt or destroy the reputation of the organisation to prove the customer right. The demand on you and the organisation, in terms of effort and resources, may far exceed what is deemed reasonable, even if you've gone that extra mile and then some. There will come a point when you will have to now be professional in another context and manage the customer expectation that you can do no more. These situations will undoubtedly be few and far between and will be exceptional as opposed to the norm. But as you will understand further when applying the PROUD model, if an exceptional situation ever arises, you will be in a better position to handle this correctly.

Summary

In summary, above all be polite and be professional at all times. Use good manners; a 'please' and a 'thank you' cost nothing. Use the customer's name; if you don't know it at the beginning, make the effort to find it out. Act professionally and do your utmost to serve the customer in the most appropriate way, realising that there may a limit to what can be reasonably achieved.

In chapter 1, we looked at a number of areas deemed important to customer service, the virtues expected by customers, along with the main theories, models, and beliefs. In being polite and professional, there are also a number of hidden aspects that you can influence right from the start:

- We are able to help set the perception of the customer—that he or she is dealing with a polite and professional individual. This forms the basis of the relationship moving forward, and, as highlighted, this can happen in the first thirty seconds.
- By creating the right perception, we can influence the customer's expectation. This can make it easier to manage expectations accordingly, as we will see later in the book.
- We are aware that behaviour can be influenced by the environment; for example, when you are talking to a doctor or other professional, you will behave differently than if you were talking to a close friend. If the perception from customers is that they are being treated politely and professionally from the outset, they will be more accommodating and adapt their behaviour accordingly.
- These tie in with behaviours and motivators around social interaction—wanting to be liked. By acting

courteously towards the customer, we can instil this aspect.
- In Kano's model, polite and professional may be the basic level expected for most customer interactions (for example, a waiter), or it may even be an unexpected delight.

So you can now see that being polite and professional from the outset is important, and again, while the PROUD model isn't a linear model, it does form a good basis for the beginning. Getting this part right will have an impact on the rest of PROUD.

Chapter 3

R: Respect

'Respect for ourselves guides our morals; respect for others guides our manners.'

Laurence Sterne, Irish-born English novelist (1713–1768)

Respect. It's a powerful word that can be used in juxtaposition: admiration of warring foes and bitter enemies, comfort and appreciation for our trusted friends and loved ones. Respect is something that is deemed a positive feeling, while the opposite, disrespect, has a negative connotation. Respect can garnish esteem or support deference. It can also be quantified: for example, a high degree of respect, a low degree of respect. Respect is something that can be given, or it can be earned; it can be taken away, and even lost. But it's not just a word. We can show respect in our gestures and through our actions as much as actually saying the word, though again, it has to be understood that different cultures view different actions and gestures in different ways. However, regardless of the culture, respect is something that is valued, and in customer service it's something that the customer values highly.

Mutual respect

Customer service is not a one-way relationship; it involves a shared understanding in order to achieve the objective or desired outcome for the customer. Without this shared understanding, it then becomes a process and, as a process, can quickly become devoid of any appreciative human interaction. In a customer service relationship, therefore, we should not think of respect as being one-way—when applied to customer service, it can be a multifaceted affair.

As we have seen, 'respect' is a complicated word used in many different ways. In customer service, there will be the type of respect paid to one's wishes or ideals; then there will be another type of respect, which has to be earned by the person dealing with the customer. Ideally, there should be mutual respect between the two parties.

If you are the person dealing with the problem, then you should respect the customer. To respect the customer primarily involves understanding the needs, wishes, and wants of the customer—his or her expectations—and dealing with these in a non-judgemental way. In other words, show the customer due regard or consideration. This does not mean that the customer is always right, as we have identified, as there may be ethical or moral issues at play.

Laurence Sterne's quote, at the start of this chapter, is used in this instance to identify that our degree of respect may negatively influence how we treat others. There may be a natural tendency to treat others that we do not respect discourteously. However, in customer service situations all customers should be treated equally, with due respect and courteously throughout. It has to be understood that a customer's request will be driven by perception and expectation. For example, if the customer wants an item in bright purple with fluorescent-green spots, who are you to judge? You need to respect the customer's wish. If asked, or if possible, you may be in a position to offer your advice. If the item can't be made in those colours, then you have to explain to the customer the logic or rationale as to why the item cannot be provided as expected. Your treatment of the customer, including your manners, must remain the same as with any customer, and that includes respecting the customer's wishes.

If you are the person dealing with the query or problem, to enhance the relationship, as well as build trust, you will need to be able to gain respect. At times you may have only a small window of opportunity in which to achieve this. If you immediately start to treat the customer courteously (politely), in a professional manner, with attention, as well as being non-judgemental, then these are the key attributes aligned to the definition of respect. If you turn this around (now you are the customer), and you are now dealing with a professional, polite individual who is being non-judgemental about you, you automatically start to regard this individual with consideration and feel more open to engaging with them. Using the example of a doctor–patient relationship, there is a degree of respect when the patient feels he or she is being dealt with by a professional, knowledgeable, and experienced individual.

Empathy

Respecting the customer also involves a degree of empathy. It needs to be understood at this point that empathy is different than sympathy. In a general context, empathy is the action or mind-set of putting yourself in another person's position and imagining or feeling what it is like; in other words, it is being emotionally connected. Sympathy is understanding and recognising another person's feelings but not being emotionally connected. I was once given the analogy of stubbing your toe. An empathetic response from someone would be 'Ouch, that must have really hurt; are you OK?' Here, there is an emotional response of feeling your pain. A sympathetic response may be 'Oh dear, are you OK?' In this response, the other person understands that you are in pain but is not feeling the full emotion.

Again, applying common sense and the Goldilocks principle, you do not want to be too empathetic, hence the earlier statement 'involves a *degree* of empathy'. For example, in the medical profession, a patient is a customer (remember: the definition of a customer is far reaching). If the doctor or nurse became too empathetic with the customers, feeling their total anguish and pain, then this would deeply affect the ability of the doctor or nurse to do his or her job. So there should be enough empathy there to care but not to consume. Again, if you are dealing with a customer who is having an emotional outburst, for example, you will be little help if you become too emotionally involved.

Summary

Despite this chapter being the shortest, respect is extremely important in the PROUD model. This is a typical case where quantity does not reflect quality or importance. In summarising this chapter, if you are polite and professional from the outset, you immediately form the foundation for gaining respect from the customer, as well as having the mind-set to respect the customer's wishes, needs, and wants.

The true value of respect is gained through the power of applying all the PROUD principles in achieving customer service excellence. As will become evident through this book, the main advantage of the PROUD model is that its sum is greater than its parts. Respect in the PROUD model runs through from start to finish, helping to bind everything together. If it didn't, the model would become more of a process, which goes against the very nature and core of PROUD.

Chapter 4

O: Own

'If you use your skill and imagination to see how much you can give for a dollar, instead of how little you can give for a dollar, you are bound to succeed!'
Henry Ford, American industrialist (1863–1947)

Throughout this book, and in your life, you will hear the term 'customer service'. The definition and explanation of this term has yet to be covered, and this is probably an opportune time to explain it in more detail. Customer service is, as the name implies, providing a service to the customer—simple. However, it's the word 'service' that we need to look at in more detail. The word 'service' itself is defined as 'an act of helpful activity; help; to do someone a service[2]'. So when providing customer service, we can say that it's helping or being helpful.

2 Oxford English Dictionary 2014

The majority of interaction with a customer revolves around the fact that the customer has a problem or issue. Whether this is directly communicated or implied, the customer's perception, and subsequently expectation, is that you will provide a service to help resolve his or her problem. The customer needs help. Although sometimes this may not be apparent at first, an angry, abusive customer may in fact be hurt (in a metaphorical way), as he or she may feel let down or as if he or she is not being taken seriously. Remember the fight-and-flight response, as well as our behavioural level of social interaction: these can combine into the 'wounded animal' syndrome. It's the feelings, emotions, or even pride that is hurt, and, in this case, the customer is adopting a fight response, striking out at anyone in his or her path.

On the other side, you may get customers who are very reticent or timid (flight response), which may give the impression that they are being awkward or uncooperative. The key thing to always remember is that you need to help the customer. Imagine the customer is a wounded animal, and you have to give the assurance that you are there to help and not to cause any harm. In essence, it is about easing the mind of the customer.

One of the best ways to do this is to take (or imply) ownership of the problem. If done correctly, this can vastly improve the customer service experience. As the quote from Henry Ford explains at the beginning of this chapter, it's about trying to be proactive with customers, helping them rather than hindering them.

Even when suggesting taking ownership of the problem, some people automatically adopt defensive responses (fight-or-flight) like 'It's a marketing problem. What do I know about marketing?' or 'I only work on the desk'. In an organisational context, high-ranking executives may recoil in horror to think that someone on reception must now be empowered to be able handle the claims account on a multimillion-pound project! But this isn't exactly what ownership is about.

Ownership is twofold. On the one hand, it's about giving the customer the confidence that his or her problem is going to be handled appropriately; on the other, it's about you adopting the mind-set of taking ownership from the outset. How the problem or issue is dealt with may vary in strategy or methodology, but at the end, the customer should feel satisfied that what could have been done was done. In some cases the outcome may not be what the customer wanted, but at least he or she will understand how and why the outcome is as it is.

And this leads to a very important point that can make or break the final part of PROUD: deliver (we will explore this concept more in chapter 6). When taking ownership with a customer, never promise something that you can't deliver. It's very tempting to get carried away at this point 'Leave it with me. I guarantee that I will sort it out' or 'I promise you that...' Taking ownership of the problem is not about making promises or guarantees—it's about giving the customer the confidence that you'll take his or her problem seriously. You want to help, but, as with life, not all outcomes can be positive or guaranteed.

Another part of PROUD that goes hand in hand with ownership is *understanding* (this will be dealt with in more detail in the next chapter). It can be reasoned that you do not want to take on a problem without fully understanding the outcome or the consequences. However, the main point here is to accept that your mind-set is open to owning the problem from the beginning. The strategies or methodologies you then use will be governed by your understanding of the problem.

Poor example

I had a personal experience (among many) of someone not taking ownership from the outset. The sales desk rep was not willing to help me with my problem, which drove this frustration home to me. A window lock on my property had broken. This was a part that could easily be removed and a new replacement part fitted by myself. The warranty had expired on the windows, and I didn't want to go to the expense of calling someone out for a job I could easily do. I duly removed the part, got the serial number from the locking mechanism, and, as the window had been purchased from a local firm, drove the short journey to their showroom. (I also wanted to meet face-to-face to improve the customer service experience as opposed calling on the phone.) This was the ensuing conversation:

Me: Hi, I wonder if you could help me.

Sales desk rep: [No response]

Me: The window lock from one of my windows that you fitted appears to have broken, and I want to replace it. I've removed it and have it here with the serial number if that's what you need.

Sales desk rep: OK. Ah, I see, unfortunately that's nothing to do with here. We just sell the windows.

Me: OK, can you tell me who I need to speak to?

Sales desk rep: Erm, no, not really, sorry. We just sell the windows. We don't have anything to do with manufacturing them, that's done elsewhere.

Me: OK, do you have a contact number or something to get hold of them?

Sales desk rep: Errmm. No, as I just said, we only sell the windows here. We don't have anything to do with manufacturing them.

Me: Right, I understand that, so who does manufacture them?

Sales desk rep: I think it's our sister company, at our depot down the road.

Me: OK. [getting slightly frustrated at this point] So, do you have a contact number for the depot?

Sales desk rep: Oh, yeah, it may be in one of our brochures.

Me: Right, so do you have a brochure with the contact details on it?

Sales desk rep: Yeah, I think so; you may find some over there behind you.

And so it went on, with me then having to sift through a couple of brochures until I found the contact details I needed. Needless to say, other people also supplied the part I needed. I determined this local firm would not be getting any repeat business from me, and I would be using the alternative suppliers in the future.

It was clear from the outset that this individual wasn't going to take ownership of my problem. He was polite, to some degree, but immediately saw this as something he had no connection to or responsibility for. Had he adopted the open mind-set of taking ownership of my problem, then my experience would have been different. He would have taken personal responsibility; this in turn would have opened him up to providing constructive dialogue. He may have offered suggestions instead of ignoring, deflecting, or passing the problem on. Had the person taken ownership of my problem, I would have felt confident that the number he gave me was the right one. Taking ownership is really a manifestation of being helpful. As described earlier, it's a mind-set that, if adopted from the outset, can really enhance a positive customer experience.

When you apply ownership or talk about ownership, it's not about taking on the other person's problem carte blanche; ownership should not be misinterpreted in this way. In the case described, I did not expect the sales desk person to sit me down with a coffee, take the item from my hand, contact the depot, get my part ordered, process my payment, and then personally deliver the part (although that would have been nice). Quite rightly, he was defending the fact that this wasn't his job (he sold windows). Contacting the depot, looking up the part, and so on would have distracted him from his main purpose—to be available to answer window-sales enquiries.

However, taking ownership involves realising that the customer has come to you with a problem—so how can you help him or her, within your scope, responsibility, and authority? In the example provided, it's clear that the sales desk person may not have been able to leave his position, but it *was* within his scope to get the information for me (he knew it was in the company brochures in his reception area). To have the attitude that 'it's not my job' clearly wasn't being helpful, nor did it give me confidence. Alternatively, the sales desk person could have said, 'We don't deal with those here, as we only sell the completed windows. You will need to speak to the manufacturing depot, which I think has a spare parts section. If you could just hold on a minute, I can get you the contact number. Right, phone this number and ask for service parts.' Had this been the case, I would have understood why he couldn't help me directly. If I had been treated in this manner, I would have felt that he'd dealt with me as a person, treated me with respect, and taken responsibility to ensure that I had a workable or viable solution to my problem, which would have given me confidence, combining to make me feel good about the whole experience. What he achieved was the opposite.

Good example

A good example of taking ownership is the time I was staying at a hotel where I was running a workshop for a major international company the following day. It was a new client, and I wanted to ensure that all went smoothly. I had never been to this hotel before. Normally I would arrive in good time to check the meeting room, layout, and equipment and be ready for the next day. In this particular case, because of transportation problems, I didn't get there until midnight. There was no function manager on duty at that time, and the night receptionist had no access to the booking paperwork or keys to the meeting room. So I decided that I would get up early in the morning, figuring I could easily check the meeting room before breakfast and still have plenty of time. In the morning, I went to reception, and upon checking with the morning receptionist and then the function manager, I was duly told that, unfortunately, the room had been double-booked. My heart sank. This was a big client with some senior people involved, and this was my first time dealing with the company. Before I had a chance to say even a word, the function manager replied, 'Sir, please accept our apology; if you would like, you can go for your breakfast, and then back to your room. Do not worry about the situation; we will make alternative arrangements. I have the details of the proposed room layout and the facilities you need. I will call you at 8:30 a.m.'

I duly went to breakfast and then back to my room. At 8:30 a.m. the internal phone rang, and it was reception asking me to return to the desk. During the time I had been at breakfast, they had emptied another meeting room that they used for storage and set everything up for my workshop. The function manager had taken ownership of my problem straightaway and dealt with it accordingly. There was no discussion as to who was at fault, no passing the problem on. The manager took ownership of the problem and resolved it to the best of her ability. The handling of the situation started from Kano's basic level, went up through performance, and continued right through to delighter.

Help

Remember, that taking ownership, or 'owning' the problem is about adopting a proactive mind-set that will lead to positive actions or words in order to help solve the initial concern. How many times have you said, as a customer, or heard the statement 'I wonder if you could help me'? This statement alone is a clear signal or request of help in some form, and if this help is not forthcoming, then immediately there is a complete disconnect with expectations and perception.

It may not be a negative problem; for example, you may be wishing to buy a car—hopefully a positive problem. In this instance the salesperson may be the one to start the conversation: 'Hi, can I help you?' Here, the implied statement is 'I'm here to help you with the probably difficult but positive experience of buying a car, as there are so many models to choose from. I'm here to offer you guidance if needed.' Understandably, there will be those cynics who say, 'No, what that salesperson is really after is a sale!' Of course that's true. But there is a high probability you are going to buy a car anyway; otherwise you wouldn't be there, and you don't have to buy from this person, so if this person can help you make the right decision, then it can make the buying experience better, now or later.

This leads to the old adage 'A problem shared is a problem halved' which also provides the basis of the mind-set of ownership. In other words, as a customer, if I believe that you are interested in my problem and have a genuine interest in helping me, I will feel better about the whole experience. There may be a sense of relief, a connection, or an understanding, all of which help to make my experience better and more enjoyable.

In order to help you will need to fully understand the problem first, which is covered in more detail in the next chapter. At all times you should try to act as an enabler to help provide possible alternatives or solutions. Never forget: it's not just the problem you have to deal with; it's the customer.

It's also important to understand that you will not have the answer to everything. A solution may be sought from others, for which you may say, 'I don't know the answer, but I know someone who does, or can help, or has experience of this.' But remember: if you are handing the problem over to someone else, then ideally, as part of the PROUD model, really excellent customer service requires that you follow up and make sure the problem was resolved to the best outcome. This, however, would be dependent on your role, organisation, and degree of empowerment. (More on this will be covered in chapter 6, 'Deliver'.)

Empowerment

In this chapter we have mentioned *empowerment* in the same context as *ownership*. It is important to understand how this interrelates with ownership. One of the many motivation models used by the empowerment movement in the workplace hails from the work of Hackman and Oldham[3] and their job enrichment motivation theory, which is used to help identify and improve job motivation. They describe five core job dimensions, which provide three critical psychological states:

- **Experienced meaningfulness (EM):** the extent to which the individual considers the work to be meaningful, valuable, and worthwhile—*What's in it for me?*

- **Experienced responsibility (ER):** the extent to which the individual feels accountable for the work output—*Who's responsible? Where does the buck stop?*

- **Knowledge of results (KR):** the extent to which individuals know and understand how well they are performing; in other words, feedback—*You're doing really well. That's a really good job.*

So, how does this relate to providing excellent customer service? Again, quite a lot, actually.

The theory proposes that people who have low experienced meaningfulness (EM) within their roles are less likely to care much about their job, as they cannot see any perceived benefit and will therefore be less likely to produce quality products or services. Similarly, autonomy is thought to affect the employees' experienced responsibility (ER), the extent to which the job holder feels personal responsibility for

---

[3] Hackman, J.R., and Oldham, G.R., *Work Redesign*, Addison-Wesley Publishing Company Inc. (1980)

the outcomes. If you are given a job where you are told that responsibility falls on you, internally you will be much more motivated to ensure that task is completed. However, if you feel that that it's someone else's responsibility, then you may be inclined to not make as much effort. It can be tempting to think, 'Well, if it all goes wrong, at the end of the day, it ain't my problem.'

Feedback (KR) is based on personal reward or reinforcement because it provides ongoing personal knowledge of how the person is performing. If there's positive or constructive feedback, then this will have a factor in increasing motivation.

Therefore, the job enrichment model implies that by taking ownership (or having the mind-set to do this), the experienced responsibility (ER) factor is increased. This may have an impact on the experienced meaningfulness (EM) factor, as 'What's in it for me?' may mean either to fail or to not fail. This combined feeling of responsibility and personal challenge may instil within the person a feeling of commitment to see the task through to a satisfactory conclusion.

But there is also a reciprocal effect to this and contributes to knowledge of results (KR). If, as a customer, I feel that the person handling my query is showing a willingness to help me with the problem, then I'm much more likely to feel that I'm being treated well, listened to, and respected, and my trust and openness increase. This should help to lead to a more satisfied customer experience. This then should be felt by the individual through the positive feedback I give (either directly or indirectly through my dialogue or behaviour). This in turn leads to increased motivation or a similar satisfying experience for the individual—a win-win for both parties.

Positive dialogue

Now that we have covered the attitudes, behaviours, and possible motivators attributed to ownership, we need to understand how these can be implied in our dialogue with the customer. Some examples of implying ownership in dialogue involve using the words 'I', 'we', and 'us' within your communication: 'Let me see what I can do. How can we help? I think I know what we need.'

Below are some suggestions for implying ownership of the problem to the customer.

Try not to say:	Try to say:
• I don't know.	• I will try to find out.
• No.	• Let's see what options are available.
• That's not my job.	• I know/will find out who can help. I will get someone to contact you/give you the contact details.
• It's not my fault.	• I understand your frustration. Let's see what…
• I'm too busy right now.	• Let me take a note of your query, and I will call you back in…
• Call me back.	• I'll call you.

The above are only suggestions; the words and phrases used should be appropriate to the context in which they are being used.

With the suggested responses, there is an implied willingness to help, but there is no mention of a guarantee or promise or of taking the problem on completely. You can only promise what you can confidently deliver. In the case of 'I will try to find out', if you are confident you can achieve this, then you may want to use 'I will find out'.

Summary

So, in summarising this chapter, ownership does not mean being left with or taking on the problem completely. Ownership predominately means having the mind-set to show customers that you are willing to help support them in achieving a satisfactory conclusion to their query, problem, or issue. It's about helping customers, taking a level of responsibility, easing their mind, giving them reassurance, confidence, and support—in other words, being helpful. Ownership is about dealing with the customer, not just the problem. This can be implied through your dialogue or subsequent actions.

Taking ownership has its roots in job enrichment theory and empowerment as key motivators. It helps to satisfy the experienced responsibility (ER) and experienced meaningful (EM) factors, as well as knowledge of results (KR) through the feedback we receive when we feel that we are doing a good job.

In some circumstances, you may not be best placed to help with the problem, and you may need to hand it over to someone who can help. In those cases, you will need to ensure that the customer is handed over and the other person takes on ownership correctly. You may also need to follow up to ensure that the customer has been dealt with properly.

The golden rule when taking ownership is that you should never promise anything that you can't deliver. Ensuring that you get this right helps to build one of the greatest requirements from a customer—trust. Trust will be further enhanced through the remainder of the PROUD model, as described in the following chapters, along with the holistic approach of PROUD itself.

Chapter 5

U: Understand

'Seek first to understand, then to be understood.'
Stephen R. Covey, American author (1932–2012)

Understand. It's a simple word yet, at times, an understated aspect within customer service. This will be the longest of the chapters within the PROUD acronym, not because we are implying this is more important than the other words within PROUD, but because of the content needed to explain this principle. This is an area that is often overlooked when taken in the context of customer service because, in some respects, there are organisations that see it as their duty to tell the customer exactly what they think the customer should do. In some cases, the organisation may have taken this stance owing to economic or commercial factors; for some, the organisation believes it knows what is best for the customer – rightly or wrongly – and doesn't fully understand the customer.

In starting this section, we need to understand what the word 'understand' is and what makes it so important within the customer service focus. 'Understanding', or 'gaining an understanding', when used in philosophical, psychological, and other associated academic works means 'intellection, intellect, or intelligence'. Other words associated with understanding include 'thought' and 'reason', as well as 'intuition' and 'awareness'. It's a process rooted in physical and abstract conceptualisation and can refer to a person, an object, or a message. To understand, or gain an understanding, requires thought to ascertain information about the particular person, object, or message, and the concepts to deal adequately with it. Understanding is a relationship between the 'knower' and the person, object, or message to be understood.

Without trying to complicate things further, there are a few more things to consider about this seemingly simple word. The basis of understanding revolves around the limit of conceptualisation—that is, the knowledge held or gained in order to interpret and construct the meaning of the person, object, or message.

For example, doctors are able to understand and diagnose a patient's condition from their knowledge about that condition, as well as information gained from questioning the patient or through observation of symptoms. From this they are able to construct a possible diagnosis and options to treat the problem. They are able to achieve this because they have knowledge about the human anatomy and how factors can affect or influence it. Those who are not medically trained (or have no previous experience of the condition) will not be able to draw the same conclusion; their level of understanding (and ability to conceptualise the issue) will be limited.

So, despite appearing as a relatively simple word, 'understand' is in fact one that has drawn the attention of the best minds throughout history and is a constant staple for philosophical debate and contemplation. However, as previously stated, this book is not written for academia. We will now start to focus on the pragmatic aspects of the word and its meaning.

Assumption

Let's first look at a lack of understanding, or other people thinking they understand without truly knowing—assumption. When this situation is applied to customer service, it can turn what appears to be excellent customer service into a bad experience.

Imagine, if you will, Mr and Mrs Smith, a middle-aged couple married for some fifteen years, with two children aged twelve and fourteen. They both work in reasonably paid jobs, and each year for the past seven years, the family has been going to the same Spanish resort for their annual all-inclusive package holiday. Branded as a 'three-star' resort in the brochure, they all love the place. It's clean, the staff are friendly, and the rooms are comfortable, with poolside views. The children are able to meet with other children their own age and make new friends, as well as reconnect with some old friends they have made over the years. The same is true for Mr and Mrs Smith, who also meet new guests as well as other regulars. The family is able to relax, enjoy good, simple food, and play by the pool during the day; in the evenings, they have a few drinks, watch the local live entertainment, and are even known to do the odd karaoke performance when the mood takes them.

Unfortunately, this year, they arrived at the resort only to find that the hotel had lost their booking, and consequently there was no reservation for them. With the hotel being fully booked at the height of the season, the staff didn't know what to do. Fortunately, the tour operator representative was on hand, and before a word could be said, she immediately took charge of the situation. All her customer service training kicked in: The customer is always right. Always go the extra mile. Under-promise and over-deliver. No quibble, no problem, no fuss. She immediately contacted the company's other hotel in the area, a five-star accommodation, which fortunately had available space.

After being ushered to the lounge with complimentary drinks in hand, the family waited for the private car that was coming to pick them up and take them to the new hotel. 'Wow,' thought Mr and Mrs Smith, 'this is very good customer service.' They were even more impressed when they turned up at the hotel and were greeted by its marble entrance way, infinity pools, and lush green gardens as their bags were whisked away to their rooms. 'This is the life,' they thought.

But within two days the Smiths were complaining to the tour representative about the hotel, the food, and the location and wanted to move back to their original hotel or one close to it. The tour representative couldn't *understand* why they were complaining. She had dealt with the problem (no quibble, no problem, no fuss) secured them an upgrade to a five-star hotel, which would have cost them four times what they originally booked. They were in luxurious surroundings; they had excellent à la carte food and large, spacious rooms with a Jacuzzi; the list goes on.

In light of all this, the tour operator representative felt that she had gone that extra mile with her customer service in the circumstances and that, rather than being thanked, she was now being criticised for her outstanding effort. Their criticism and her behaviour thereon was to dismiss the Smiths as being ungrateful.

On returning home, the Smiths filed a formal complaint with the tour operator, citing the trip as being the worst holiday they'd ever been on, and they also went on every travel review site to post their comments. Again, there was some bemusement from the organisation as to why they were complaining.

However, when someone took the time to listen and understand the reason for the Smiths' complaint, it became clear that the organisation, despite providing the standard excellent customer service, hadn't taken the time to *understand* what kind of holiday the Smiths wanted.

Being in a five-star hotel situated on the edge of the town meant that they were cut off from any social nightlife and some of their old friends. The only way to get to town was by taxi, the drivers of which charged extortionate fares as they thought everyone in the hotel must be extremely well off. There were no other children at the hotel, so the Smith children got bored very quickly, and it isn't good having two bored teenagers around. Meal times were also problematic as the children didn't like the menu, and they couldn't just wander into the restaurant wearing shorts and T-shirts, as they could in the other hotel. These, along with other issues, turned the holiday into one that they would not forget, but for all the wrong reasons.

This story is meant to highlight that the standard customer service messages—the customer is always right, always go the extra mile, under-promise and over-deliver—can only work effectively if you understand what is needed. Only then can you take the appropriate action. In this scenario the representative assumed she knew what would make the situation better and made the decisions needed without understanding what was actually wanted. Sometimes, in the right context and in the right situation, the 'I know best' approach can sometimes work (remember Henry Ford's reputed quote, 'If I had asked the people what they wanted, they would have said faster horses'). However, in this case, Stephen Covey's quote at the beginning of this chapter, 'Seek first to understand, then to be understood,' sums up the key message. To gain knowledge, we have to understand; without understanding, the message, person, or object cannot be conceptualised correctly. This then leads to errors.

Engage

In essence, for you to truly understand another person, you need to engage with that person. There has to be dialogue, whether it is face-to-face or through other media. You need to engage with the other person to get to the heart of his or her perception in order to manage his or her expectation. This book is not meant to teach you the skills or techniques required for engagement; there are many books, workshops, and training programmes in this area. However, in order to engage with the other person, there are two basic key requirements that you need and that you need to master: to listen and to ask questions. Encompassing both of these is the important aspect of context, as this helps to correctly frame the information gained from questioning and listening.

Listen

Take listening first. It's one of the most highlighted topics in communication, interpersonal, coaching, and mentoring programmes and workshops. Whole industries rely on good listeners and their ability to listen well, yet listening is something that most people do very poorly. While most people do listen, they may not listen enough or listen correctly. It's a skill, it's an art, and it's something that we have to do actively if we really want to listen correctly.

The following statement is often attributed to Epictetus, the Greek philosopher (AD c. 55–135) surmising the importance of listening as: 'We have two ears and one mouth so we can listen twice as much as we speak.' If this was highlighted nearly two-thousand years ago, why are we still so poor at it? Listening takes time, as well as patience, which to some may be difficult to sustain owing to our fast-paced here-and-now lifestyles. Everyone is in a hurry, but sometimes, taking the time out to actually listen can pay dividends in the long run as your understanding improves and mistakes and corrections are minimised.

But how can we listen better? The key is that you have to make yourself *want* to listen. I was once asked a question at a workshop I attended as delegate: 'When do you really listen?' I thought about the question and tried to answer as best I could with a couple of fairly weak examples, not articulating them as well as I should have. (It was like being asked to describe an elephant—I know what it is and what it looks like, but describing it properly is more difficult.) The facilitator listened to my answers, smiled, and said, 'Thank you for those and they are good examples, but I would like to suggest another example. A time when you really, and I mean really, listen is around two in the morning. You've been disturbed in your sleep by a noise. Immediately upon wakening, your whole being is focusing in on the atmosphere and the sounds around you. That's an example of when you are truly listening!' I sat back and realised that yes, that's what I had wanted to say!

Listening is different from hearing. Hearing is the mechanical process that goes on when sound reaches your ear: the interaction between the eardrum, the bones and fluid in the cochlear, and the nerve. Listening is taking this and applying cognitive reasoning to make sense of the sounds being heard.

There is a further degree of listening, which is termed 'active' listening. Active listening (and a good example of this was the facilitator's middle-of-the-night scenario) involves more than just hearing and listening. It involves, as the facilitator mentioned in his example, taking in other cues or, in his words, picking up on the 'atmosphere' as well. So active listening is the higher, cerebral action of listening when other factors come into play. These may include picking up on the tone or pitch of voice, non-verbal gestures or body language cues, the environment, and the elimination of superfluous background noise.

Here is another example of active listening. Humans have a reasonably good auditory capacity, not in the same range as some other animals, but certainly good enough for most of our needs. It is amazing that when you are in a crowded, fairly noisy place, like a bar or restaurant, if someone mentions your name, say from another table, you can instantly switch from listening to the conversation around you and focus on the area where you heard your name being mentioned. You then concentrate on the other conversation, straining to hear what is being said. If it's within earshot, then you can cut out some of the other interfering noises around you. This, again, is an example of active listening, and it highlights the capacity we have to focus in and concentrate on what is being said.

But having now realised that we are capable of this, why don't we do it more often? There are many factors to consider. These examples of active listening highlight some of the more important points, but the one common factor is that we have *reasons* to listen to what is being said:

- It's scary—what is being said causes feelings of fear or threatens us.
- It's important—what is being said could have a beneficial or detrimental effect on us.
- It's personal—what is being said may have an impact on us, either positive or negative.
- It's enjoyable—what is being said is favourable to us.
- It's educational or interesting.

Another point to note is that active listening is tiring. You listen all the time, constantly taking in noises and sounds. Normal listening is like taking a gentle stroll, just meandering along, taking in the views, without a care in the world. Then, suddenly, if you have a situation that requires active listening (a noise at night, your name mentioned in a crowded room), you automatically step up a gear or two, as though something has startled you, and you suddenly go off into a focused, determined sprint. All your energy and focus is now concentrated in listening mode. However, you cannot sustain this sprint indefinitely, so when the situation is over, or your mind starts to get tired because of the extra activity, you then resort to strolling, or passive listening. People who are good listeners are like long-distance runners; they have practiced and trained to step it up a gear when needed and are usually able to sustain the pace for longer.

Being aware of your limitations can help when you are in the process of actively listening. If you feel that you are losing concentration, take a break, make an excuse, catch your breath, and then continue to actively listen when you're refreshed. Trying to push on at this time will prove detrimental both to you and the person you are listening to. While we all have the capability to actively listen, it's sometimes our capacity that can let us down. As with all skills, in order to increase our capacity, as well as our capability, we need to practice.

Therefore, active listening is creating the mind-set that you *want* to listen, that there is a reason for you to listen. The speaker (customer) should feel that you are giving him or her your undivided attention. To help with this, remember these rules:

1. Take in the whole atmosphere:

    - Eliminate background noise. Find a quiet, accessible place to talk. Ensure you and other parties are comfortable with the surroundings.

- Look for non-verbal cues and body language: fidgeting, playing with objects, eye contact, and so forth.
- Listen to the speaker's tone, pitch, and volume. Note any changes or variations.
- Think about what was *not* said. Is the speaker saying one thing, but other clues are indicating that there may be more? Maybe the speaker is not being fully truthful or is holding back.

2. Be aware of the following:

   - Your body language, your non-verbal cues. Are you acting defensively, or are you acting interested? In other words, are you maintaining adequate eye contact, but not staring at the speaker too much, nor averting your gaze all the time? Are you smiling in a genuine way?
   - Your tone, pitch, and volume. Don't raise your voice, even if the speaker does—this can escalate problems and possible conflict.
   - Your memory. You can only take in a certain amount of information at any one time. Remember that true active listening requires a lot of mental energy, and you may become tired or lose concentration, so don't be afraid to take notes.

3. Interact with the other person:

   - Ask questions to gain understanding.

- Summarise or paraphrase back to the person what you've heard or understood.
- Ensure that the person understands that you want to listen to him or her.

These final points lead us into the second part of understanding, and that's asking questions.

Questions

The power of questions cannot be underestimated. Many of you will have heard this statement: 'Ask a poor question and get a poor answer.' Voltaire (an eighteenth-century French writer and philosopher) said, 'Judge a man by his questions, not by his answers.'

When running management workshops, I often use a quote that I acquired from another trainer, and it goes: 'Knowing answers means asking questions; asking the right questions is the art of management.' Where the other trainer got this quote I don't know, but I always thought it was very poignant. There are two key elements contained in this statement—you gain knowledge and understanding from asking questions, and there is a right and a wrong way to ask questions.

Young children seem to start every sentence with 'why'. Why? Because they need to understand and learn what they can and cannot do, what is good, what is bad, and 'what happens if…'. They are constantly trying to work out and understand the world they live in. And they believe that you have the answer. However, they are not able to fully articulate this using other forms of questions, so 'why?' serves its purpose well, for now.

But there are other words and other styles we can use to ask questions.

The famous author Rudyard Kipling wrote the following verse (taken from a poem called 'Six Honest Serving Men' in the book *The Elephant's Child*):

> I kept six honest serving men,
> (They taught me all I knew);
> Their names are: What and Why and When,
> And How and Where and Who.

Kipling was right. These 'men' do serve you well, as they are the basis for what are called 'open' questions. Open questions can be used for many purposes:

- Invite the person to expand upon his or her answer: *What makes you say that? What are your best options to move this forward?*
- Get the person talking: *When did you start to feel like this?*
- Gain specific information: *How long has this been going on? What house do you live at? What speed was your car doing at the time?*
- Form the framework of an investigative process: *Who was involved? What happened? Where did it take place? When did it take place? Why did it happen? How can this be prevented?*

Sometimes—and again, this has to be taken in context—the 'why' question should be used with a slight caveat. Why?

Well, as indicated, our first experience of this word is as very young children: we use this word to gain understanding and knowledge of our new world. However, the next major introduction to 'why' occurs in our later childhood/teenage years, this time being said by other people *to* us, usually those in authority: 'Why haven't you tidied your room? Why haven't you done your homework? Why didn't you…?' This introduction to 'why' is usually negative. This can instil within us negative subconscious feelings. Later in our years when we are asked 'why', it can invoke those feelings again. So if you ask someone, 'Why did you do it that way?' your intention may be genuine and you may want to be helpful, but be aware that your inquiry may be perceived in a different context by the person hearing the question. Because of these subconscious references, the person may suddenly feel that you are being critical of his or her approach, and you may notice a corresponding change in the atmosphere.

The opposite of open questions is closed questions. As the name suggests, these can hinder or close a conversation down (but this also has to be taken in context, which will be explained further). Generally they are used to gain a precise answer: either yes or no. Closed questions usually start with the words *do*, *did*, *have*, and *are*, among others. Here are some examples of these:

- Do you live in London?
- Did you see the football match last night?
- Have you lived here long?
- Are you going to the shops?

Here, the response can be a straight yes or no, with no further explanation required. However, responses to closed questions can also be influenced by your relationship and rapport with the customer. Consider the football question above: if I was asked this by a complete stranger in the street, my answer would be a straight yes or no. (I would also probably be feeling a little anxious as to why I was being asked!) If the same question was asked by a good friend of mine while in a relaxed social atmosphere, then my response would different, perhaps, 'Yes, wasn't it an absolute farce, the ref...', and my friend may have trouble trying to shut me up! Despite being asked the same question, I responded in different ways.

Other uses of closed-type questions, but again taking into account the degree of relationship, are as follows:

- To confirm information: *Have I got that right?*
- To move the conversation along: *Can we continue?*
- To close a conversation down: *Have we finished?*

There are many other forms and types of questions and degrees of application (hypothetical, reflective, rhetorical), each with its own uses and limitations, and it's not the intention of this book to go into detail about the varying forms. Open and closed questions are the basic fundamental styles of questions that we need to be aware of, and an understanding of these will serve us well. There is, however, one other question format we need to look at, and that is the 'leading' question.

Leading questions are asked in a way that 'forces' or guides the other person into answering in a particular way, usually to gain a response that is expected by the person asking the question: 'You do like coffee, don't you? I am sure that you will agree that this is the best way, isn't it?' These kinds of questions generally start as closed-style questions, but end with an added emphasis: 'Don't you? Isn't it? Aren't you?' These can be seen as overpowering or even bullying in some situations.

You should be wary of asking leading questions in customer service situations, as it may give the impression that you are forcing the issue or trying to put someone on the back foot. If the situation is a little volatile, or getting that way, this type of question may be the spark that ignites the flames of hostility. So, as with listening, if you notice a change in the atmosphere during the conversation, then think—was it something you might have said?

When asking questions, we are aiming to gather information that we can use to understand the situation better. As humans we are a cybernetic system, consisting of an interconnected mind and body, and, as such, we need feedback to operate. This feedback, whether it's gathered through listening, asking questions, or observing our environment and gauging the atmosphere, helps us to gain clarity on what's going on around us. If our feedback is free from distortion, then our responses and judgement are far better.

Check and clarify

The final point to be made here concerning questions is that you should never be afraid to check and clarify. This hails back to *assumption*. If you clarify things with the customer, then it helps to prevent any misunderstanding between you. It also shows that you were listening and can give the added impression of reassurance; you are trying to get it right. When you check and clarify, you summarise back to the person your *understanding* of the situation. This helps to prevent any ambiguity or assumptions from either party.

Context

We identified listening and asking questions earlier as two of the most important requirements of understanding. We also have to factor in another aspect of understanding your customer, and that is *context*.

Context is described as 'the circumstances that form the setting for an event, statement, or idea, and in terms of which it can be fully understood'.[4] It is sometimes referred to as the 'bigger picture' or 'setting the scene', dependant on the circumstances. Context also forms part of the construct with perception, being a formation of ideas and information and, from this, forming an opinion. As we already discussed in earlier chapters, perception can also play a major part in expectation. Focusing back on the definition of context from the dictionary, 'it can be fully understood' highlights the importance of being able to understand. If we want to be able to understand our customer, then listening and questioning are the skills we need to employ, but context is the aspect that pulls, binds, frames, and makes sense of the problem or issue.

Example

As an example of this, I sometimes refer back to an incident that happened to me a few years back. I took my car to get fixed. It had a small problem with the fuel injection, but this was not the full problem, as I will explain. The mechanic, being very keen and eager to demonstrate his expert knowledge, started to deal with me in the way he thought best. He was polite and professional (so far so good), he was respectful in his approach, he took ownership of the problem ('Let's see what I can do. We will look at.... I will...' and so forth), and he tried to apply

4 *Oxford English Dictionary* (2014)

understanding (he listened and asked a couple of questions)—all going well so far.

But what he failed to do was to look at the bigger picture and put my problem into context. Needless to say, when I got the call that the car was fixed, I went round to pick it up. The injection system had been overhauled, but this was not the overreaching problem. You see, during my conversation with the mechanic, he had locked onto the fuel injection system (he appeared to be very technically minded, and an intricate problem like this was far more interesting to him than a mundane oil or tyre change). What he had failed to take into account was the bigger-picture problem. I had told him that during the course of a previous journey, I had run the tank dry, and I suspected that sludge or debris from the bottom of tank may have caused the problem. Needless to say, he concentrated only on the fuel injection system, as this was intricate and precise and something that excited him, and didn't bother to clean or replace the other fuel filters farther back in the system. So, as soon as I drove off the forecourt and got a couple of miles down the road, the problem started again.

Doctors and nurses are taught to take a 'holistic' view of the patient, to ask questions not just about the problem the patient is describing but about other aspects as well, such as lifestyle, the situation in which the problem happened, history, timelines—basically, an inquisitive type of dialogue. This is to ensure that they understand the context of the symptoms, which in turn will play an important role in giving the right treatment for the good of the patient.

Putting things into context and understanding the situation and how this can go wrong leads us to what has been described as the 'world's funniest joke' (as based on Richard

Wiseman's, University of Herefordshire, research in 2002, as part of an Internet experiment called LaughLab).

> Two hunters are out in the woods when one of them collapses. He doesn't seem to be breathing, and his eyes are glazed. The other guy whips out his phone and calls emergency services. He gasps, 'My friend is dead! What can I do?' The operator says, 'Calm down. I can help. First, let's make sure he's dead.' There is a silence, then a gunshot is heard. Back on the phone, the guy says, 'OK, now what?'

Summary

When dealing with your customer, you need to understand your customer: his or her needs, wants, and expectations. To do this, you need to ensure that you listen—and particularly, listen actively—to what is being said, taking in the atmosphere as well as other social and environmental signals.

As we have seen, questions are also key to learn and understand. Asking the right questions is important, but of equal importance is creating the right environment and atmosphere. If customers are at ease, their response and willingness to come forward with information increases, as does their trust in you.

You should also be aware of ensuring that the questions you ask involve context. This means ensuring that you take a holistic, bigger-picture approach to ensure that the customer's query or request is not a small part of a much bigger problem. Putting the customer's query into context and not just focusing on one small aspect can aid the full understanding of the problem. Remember, it's not just the problem you need to consider but the customer as well.

Chapter 6

D: Deliver

> 'Customers don't expect you to be perfect. They do expect you to fix things when they go wrong.'
> *Donald Porter, CBE, former vice president of British Airways*

The last part of PROUD is 'deliver'. Ultimately, your goal is to ensure that you deliver on the expectation of the customer. Delivery is about ensuring that the overall experience of customers, from start to finish, meets their basic needs at the minimum and ultimately provides the delight factor. The analogy I use when running workshops is what I call the 'ta-da! moment', where the magician reveals the last part of the trick, to the amazement of the audience. Like the magician, you have engaged with the customer and built rapport, trust, and understanding, and now comes the finale, which requires you to complete the customer service journey through PROUD.

Again, one of the common sayings that you will hear in the customer service world is to 'under-promise and over-deliver'. The key part with delivery, as stated earlier in the chapter on ownership, is to never promise something you can't deliver. Never guarantee that your customers will get what they want from the outset; it may be that during the understanding phase, it becomes evident that the customers' expectation is far greater than you imagined. You then have the very difficult task of trying to manage this expectation: you've promised something that you now realise you can't deliver. You can offer only that which is within your control.

It's important to point out at the outset that 'deliver' does not always mean having to deliver a positive outcome. In an ideal world, this would be the case, and it's something that you should always aspire to achieve for the customer. The main thing to remember is that you are also managing expectations, and having got to this stage, you should have a greater understanding of the expectation of the customer.

Regardless of whether the outcome is positive or negative, there is an expectation from the customer that there will be some form of end delivery. Whatever the outcome, there must be a conclusion, closure to the situation. This expectation needs to be addressed, and it's something you can't ignore. You cannot leave your customer hanging, waiting for an answer or with an incomplete response. Like with the magician, the audience wants to see the man sawn in half, the lady disappear, the rabbit pulled out of the hat.

Ignore this basic fact at your peril. You may have done all you can to resolve the customer's problem, spent precious time and effort in doing so, and realised you cannot give the answer you think the customer wants to hear, so you may feel that no response is better than a negative response. Wrong. There is nothing more insulting than to be ignored, and one way to give this impression is not following up or denying a response when expected.

Information

Take again, for example, the medical world: the customer is the patient. Applying the PROUD principle, we can see that in general, medical staff are polite and professional. They will respect the patient's wishes, take ownership, take the time to understand, and conclude with an appropriate treatment or prognosis. Their profession is one of the classic examples where they have to deliver the outcome, whether good or bad. The most common phrases doctors and nurses will hear are 'Tell me straight. I need to know. What's the prognosis?' or similar. There is a need within us to have information; armed with information, we then can make choices and take appropriate measures. Without information we can't make choices—which in turn can add to our frustration and anxiety. So it is the duty of the doctor or nurse to deliver the outcome, whether good or bad. Whether they want to do this is immaterial.

Delivery, as we have seen, cannot be ignored, even if the outcome is not a positive one. As Donald Porter's quote highlights, we are not perfect; we make mistakes, and we are fallible—but we must deliver. There is always an expectation from the customer that the problem or issue will be resolved or dealt with appropriately. There may be external or internal factors that constrain actions beyond our control and so limit our ability to deliver, but the customer needs to be made aware of these.

'...then to be understood.'

As mentioned in the previous chapter (chapter 5, 'Understand'), the first part of Stephen Covey's quote, 'Seek first to understand', was used to highlight this topic area. The second part of the quote, 'then to be understood', is now used to amplify and connect understanding to delivery. When trying to deliver on a customer's expectation, keep in mind that it is precisely that—an expectation. So we need to be able to manage the customer's expectation. It is key that the expectation of the customer must be understood. When we understand what this expectation is, and to what extent, if we have applied the PROUD principle (in particular the skills and techniques of understanding), we will have a much clearer picture. Through this understanding, we are now in a much better position to manage that expectation in order to deliver what is needed.

Another fact to consider is that delivery is also strongly linked with taking ownership. Taking on the mind-set of ownership of the problem (as we have seen from Hackman and Oldham) helps to make you more receptive to finding a solution to the problem. This eagerness will show the customer that you are trying, or have tried, to resolve the outcome to the best of your ability.

Solution

It's at this point that, having applied the PROUD principles, you will be in a better position to gain agreement with the decision or be in a position to facilitate a more acceptable solution. Once you have provided polite, professional behaviour, shown respect, taken ownership of the problem or issue, and sought to understand the problem, you will have gone a great way towards building trust and mutual respect with the customer. Even if you can't fix the problem, you can offer alternatives or a reason as to why it can't be fixed.

In an ideal world, the solution or decision would be exactly or near to what the customer wants, but there will be occasions when your response may not be what the customer expected, and he or she may not agree with the outcome. Having gone through PROUD, these occasions will hopefully be few and far between. If this does occur, however, one important point to remember is not to take the customer's grievance personally, as it is more likely a manifestation of frustration with the situation or problem itself (remember the wounded animal scenario). Because you have adopted the PROUD principles, the customer will realise that he or she is dealing with a polite, professional, respectful, and helpful individual who has taken the time to listen and understand, as well as propose a viable solution. In other words, you're on their side. This will more than likely cause customers to rein in any unwarranted behaviour, as they will (possibly reluctantly) now have a better understanding of why the decision or outcome has been reached. Through this understanding they will realise that you are not the barrier; other factors are, including possibly their own expectations.

Deliver to others

There may also be times when you personally can't deliver what's expected. This may be owing to a number of factors beyond your control, which could include authority, level of seniority required, capability, or required competence. Again, if you personally are unable to resolve the customer's issue, then do not leave the customer wanting. Good delivery does not mean just passing the problem on without due care.

As we stated in the chapter on ownership, you are still responsible for ensuring that the customer is treated correctly. It should be your responsibility to direct the customer to someone who is capable of dealing with the problem or, if not, able to direct the customer to the required information. Both you and the customer should feel confident that, if you have to undertake this course of action, he or she will not be left alone to flounder or handed over to someone who isn't capable of taking care of the problem. Using the medical profession again as an example, as a patient (customer), if I go to see a doctor at a medical centre and the doctor is unable to help me, then the doctor will refer me to a specialist.

Again, in the case of the scenario I had with my window locks (see chapter 4), the person in question didn't deliver. It could be argued that he did deliver me the required information by telling me that the details I needed were in the company brochures. But that meant that I then had to spend time and effort to retrieve that information, which he could easily have given me.

Follow-up

In some situations you may want to follow up with customers to ensure that their query or issue was dealt with correctly and appropriately under the circumstances. This encompasses the PROUD principles of being professional, respectful, taking ownership, understanding, and delivering the outcome. Delivery is about gaining satisfactory closure.

There is no set time limit for when this closure will occur, and it may be that the problem or issue goes on for some time, in which case it may require follow-up actions until closure is achieved.

Summary

The last piece of the PROUD principle, 'deliver', is about ensuring that you do not leave your customer without an end result, or closure. It's important to highlight that you can deliver only on what you are able to under the circumstances. There may be some degree of discrepancy between the customer's expectation and what can actually be achieved. Having gone through the PROUD principle—being polite and professional, respecting the customer, taking ownership, and understanding the customer through active listening and questioning—you will be better placed to manage those expectations and deliver appropriately. The outcome may not be a positive one, but at this stage the customer should understand your rationale, and, while they may not initially agree, you need to remember not to take their frustration personally.

Personal delivery—that is, personally dealing with customers' problems or queries and reaching a solution—is ideal. However, there may be times when you have to involve others in order to achieve delivery. In these situations, you have to ensure that the handover is conducted correctly. The customer has to feel confident through the whole PROUD customer experience.

Chapter 7

Be PROUD: *Achieving Excellent Customer Service*

Having read through this book, you will have gained an insight into the concept and principle of PROUD, as a framework, mind-set, ethos, and philosophy that aims to help you achieve excellent customer service. It can provide the basis of a culture, 'the way we do things here', which can be embodied by all members of an organisation, not just those who are classed as traditional customer-facing personnel. Every one of us at some time is a customer, and every one of us at some time will deal with customers. This is irrespective of where you are in the organisation; it affects everyone from the office cleaner to the CEO. PROUD applies to all levels, and not just within an organisation but within our personal lives as well.

Individually, each word used to form PROUD describes powerful attributes and behaviours that we would expect from excellent customer service and engagement, but when united, the words form an even more powerful alliance. When combined into an acronym—PROUD—they create one of the most powerful and emotive words in the English language. It's a philosophy of 'the whole is greater than the sum of its parts'.

As previously stated, while at first the PROUD acronym may appear that it should follow a linear process (that is, start with P, then R, then move onto O, and so on), this is not entirely true. PROUD should be viewed as a holistic model, dependent on the context to which it is being applied.

As we have seen, if you respond to your customer in a polite and professional manner, this implies a degree of respect, which is further enhanced as you move through PROUD. Providing polite and professional service helps to satisfy the basic needs, wants, and motivators within the customer (for example, social and esteem motivators). This helps to build rapport, as well as create a degree of openness. With these courteous, attentive behaviours, there will be an implied sense of mutual respect, both to the customer and to you. In taking, or implying, ownership of the problem through your mind-set, actions, and dialogue, it helps to further increase the feeling of openness and increased rapport, as well as build the relationship and, more importantly, the basis of trust. In addition, this can increase your willingness to help solve the problem (whether directly or indirectly), which the customer will pick up through your positive actions or words.

Listening to the customer, asking questions, and seeking to understand the problem will help to facilitate the final part. The final part is delivery; whether this is a positive or negative outcome, you will be better equipped to explain the situation: what has been done to resolve the problem, any options available, and an agreement on possible solutions. If the delivery is beyond your control, then adapt to this direction, ensuring that the customer is provided with the appropriate support, whether this is a source of information or another person.

At the end of this experience, customers should *feel* as though they have received a personalised service, increasing their positive customer service experience, which enhances Maya Angelou's important quote. They will also have experienced behaviours and feelings aligned to trust, openness, integrity, and respect, all of which the customer deems important.

The PROUD model and its construct are supported through the use of behavioural as well as psychological models and theories. These are used to explain as well as support the use of each word. We have seen how, for example, an understanding of basic motivational principles provides explanations for some of the words. Even without these, there is a common-sense understanding. We know these things happen, or we feel them. In relating PROUD across customer service models (for example, Kano's model), we can see that adopting PROUD builds from establishing basic needs (polite and professional), to increased performance (respect, ownership, and understanding), to helping provide delighters (delivery).

The PROUD model was not born from years of studious academic research or from an unquestionable depth of data. It professes only to provide a workable and common-sense approach to adopt when providing customer service. However, to justify its use, there is evidence to support the rationale behind its formation.

The adoption of PROUD will ensure that you have a principle to follow that will help you and your organisation achieve excellent customer service. It is not a rigid model or axiom, and the PROUD principle can be modified to suit the needs of any situation. One of its unique properties is that it can be applied to any customer situation in any sector, discipline, or profession organisationally, or even in your personal life.

It encompasses the main virtues of applying excellent customer service, using proficient individual words to form a single word, a universally powerful acronym, for which there is no equal.

As previously stated, we are all at times customers, and we also deal with customers, regardless of our positions. The next time you are dealing with a customer, step back and ask yourself, 'Am I being PROUD?'

Polite and **Professional** at all times, having

Respect for the customer; taking

Ownership of the problem; gaining an

Understanding of a customer's needs and wants; ensuring you

Deliver on what is possible.

About the author:

John has worked internationally in senior management positions in consultancy, SMEs, and corporate FTSE 100 companies. These have included a diverse array of industries and sectors ranging from engineering, energy, and aerospace through to tourism.

During his career he has designed, developed, and delivered numerous management, leadership, and soft-skills programmes in areas including customer focus, customer engagement, and customer service.

John holds an MA in human resource development, is a fellow of two leading UK leadership and management institutes, and is a professional engineer. He is a qualified executive coach and leadership mentor, as well as a psychometric and occupational assessor.

John provides a range of professional learning and development consultancy services, as well as PROUD – Achieving Customer Service Excellence workshops through his company, PMR Training and Development Ltd.

www.pmrtraining.co.uk

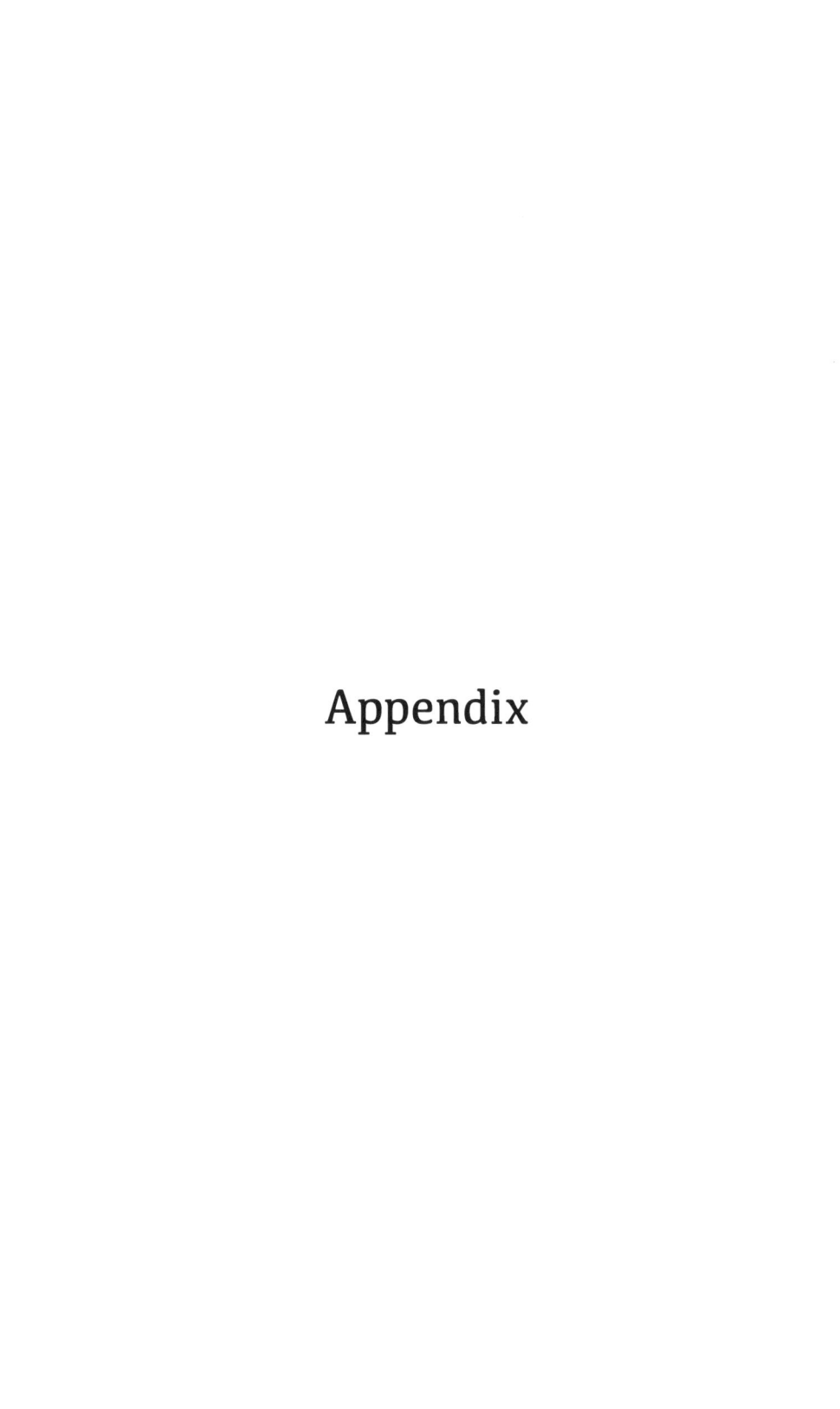

Appendix

Appendix

Having attended as a delegate, and having also delivered many customer service orientated programmes and workshops, the regular words that kept (and still do) coming up in flip-chart exercises, discussions and exercises around customer service include:

respect, trust, manners, polite, courteous, responsibility, delivery, using your name, listening, understanding, empathy, being treated as an individual, asking questions, deliver on their promise, not being left hanging on, integrity, trust, morals, ethics, taking responsibility, helping, assisting, providing solutions – not problems, friendly...

There are many, many more but these were the main ones that kept reoccurring, and still do.

If these were the key words or phrases that customers wanted from excellent customer service - then why couldn't they be grouped or arranged into an acronym, or statement, or model that was easy to remember and to use? So PROUD was formed.

Grouping these words and phrases under the main letters of PROUD we can see how they fully support each of the individual letters and main words forming PROUD:

Polite & Professional – e.g.

- Manners
- Being courteous
- Using names
- Being treated as a person
- Friendly
- Morals
- Ethics
- Standards

Respect – e.g.

- Having due regard
- Deference
- Courteous
- Integrity
- trust

Own – e.g.

- Easing the mind
- Being helpful
- Taking responsibility
- Mind-set of wanting to help
- Using positive pro-active language
- Being pro-active
- Assisting

Understand – e.g.

- Taking the time
- Listening – really listening
- Asking the right questions
- Looking at the bigger picture

Deliver – e.g.

- Deliver on their promise
- Know the outcome – good or bad
- Following up
- Handing over to someone that understands
- Not being left in the dark/un-answered questions
- Delivering solutions – not further problems

You can see why the statement that PROUD is probably the only customer service acronym that you will ever need, as it:

- satisfies all the main areas, words and phrases within the customer service genre
- covers the whole customer service journey from start to finish
- uses easy, practical language
- makes common sense
- can be used in any situation, organisation or profession; and above all
- forms the ultimate word - that if you get the customer service right – you should feel immensely **proud** of your efforts.

Printed in Great Britain
by Amazon